Thirsty
customers
coming in

Table of Contents

Foreword

Some background on where I work and who I am. I am 40 (2013) years old and was born in Belize, the former British Honduras. I have been a professional bartender for about 20 years. I am currently the bartender for Tobacco Caye Lodge in Belize. As can be seen from the photo on the book cover, my bar is not what is typically found in most resorts or large hotels. I consider it a small piece of paradise.

Tobacco Caye is a unique little island that sits directly on a barrier reef. It is unique because this island operates like a little village (the whole island is only about 5 acres with no motorized vehicles). You can always find a lot of friendly locals. In other words, we are just like one big happy family and all of us try to make sure you have an unforgettable time on your visit.

The other side of the Caye showing some of the dead coral washed up from the barrier reef.

Captain Buck picking up some folks from the dock. A catamaran with some sailors aboard is in the background.

The way we treat you, our guests, truly comes from our hearts as Belizeans. We're sure that you are gonna want to keep coming back just as hundreds of others do. It is easy for one to fall in love with Belize and its people. Tobacco Caye is a half way point between Placencia and Caye Caulker. So every marine vessel travelling back and forth from those Cayes stops in, either to have a drink or for an over night stay. On a regular day we may have five or six catamarans in our harbor, and it's usually older folks. They normally all come ashore in the evenings to have a cocktail and most times it turns into a party. It is just one more beautiful day on Tobacco Caye—the wind is coming from the east at 10-15 knots. The sun is extremely bright and from where I sit in the bar I am able to see roughly 50% of the island. The second largest barrier reef in the world is directly in front of me. I am surrounded by multiple colors of crystal clear water of the Caribbean Sea. The island is fairly quiet at this time, around noon, which is when I start my work day.

Boat with some tourists at the end of the dock. The bar is to the left. The official guard dog is under the tree.

The beach is lined with beautiful girls in bikinis and I am here talking with my friends from Canada who are whining about how it is cold back home—as we sit in paradise on Tobacco Caye. Being a bartender is amazing to me because I love what I do. Most of the time it does not even feel like a job. There are times I don't even want to go to work because I'm feeling tired or burned out, but as soon as I smell the liquor, cigarette smoke and the sound of the music hits me, it is amazing how fast I become energized and ready to work.

It is Saturday afternoon and the bar is prepped and ready. I am playing soft reggae music on my stereo patiently awaiting the Raga Muffin tour boat to arrive; they should get here around 2:00 o'clock. They usually arrive with about 20 guests for an overnight stay. They are all campers and have to set up their tents. As soon as they arrive I turn up the music to get the party started. We usually have live drummin on nights like this. It's usually a hyper party night, lots of drinking, dancing—fun people having a blast on the Caye.

Please Keep The Noise Down!!

It is exciting for me because I meet people from all walks of life and without any effort at all. I get to know who they are, where they are from and what they do. In a short period of time I usually make a lot of friends, some long term. I have even had a couple invite me to Alaska—in the winter!

It was challenging for me, especially, when I used to work night clubs, to deal with the different vibes in the club. For instance, when walking over to a customer, I have to quickly figure out if he or she is in a good or bad mood while taking their order. At the same time I adjust my (P.R) public relations skills in a way that is not noticeable to the customer, which instills respect and a friendly atmosphere. The right approach helps me to remain in control of my surroundings.

One of the fun things about being a bartender on Tobacco Caye is meeting interesting people from all over the world. For instance two of our guests arrived and they made their way over to the bar and started chatting in English then I found out that they were from Africa. We were talking about how things operate in Belize. Then about five or six of the local guys came over and I turned and started talking to them in Creole. The couple from Africa understood every word we were saying in Creole! We were amazed by it and asked how they knew what we were talking about, they then explained that back home they speak African Creole which is slightly different from Belizean Creole but we still understood each other well. For their entire stay we had an awesome time with them because we started comparing the African Creole and the Belizean Creole.

Over the years I have had numerous customers ask for one or more of my drink recipes. I have also had many ask how do you become a bartender?, why don't you do a book on your drinks?, and how do you run a bar? These questions have been asked so many times that I have decided to do a small book. There are literally hundreds of bar books and guides, but mine will be a bit unique as it will have drinks that I have found or invented that are designed for an island bar in this part of the Caribbean. Naturally, over the years I have learned a lot of to dos and not to dos in running a bar. I am including my observations in a chapter at the end of this book.

I have some friends from Alaska who have visited Tobacco Caye once a year for the past seven years. They admire our weather and talk about how much they love it here. Then they told me how cold it is back home and that they can take a hot cup of coffee and throw it outside and it would freeze before it hits the ground. Then "say Kirk you should come visit us someday" to which I replied, "are you trying to figure out how fast I would freeze?"

Kirk Westby's recipe section of this book is divided into four sections:

Section one: Is designed for non-alcohol customers, they are all virgin drinks.

Section two: Is designed for customers who would like to be introduced to alcohol for the first time. These cocktails are designed to hide the alcohol taste for those just starting out or don't like a strong alcohol flavor.

Section three: Is a series of standard cocktails for regular customers who already know what it feels like to get a buzz. As a bartender section three will be your most active section.

Section four are my Signature Drinks which are also known as "Sudden Death."

You will find that you'll be making these drinks a lot. Since this is the most active part of this book you would want to learn these standard drinks first. From that point it is easy to go back and forth to other sections, depending on the customer's needs. Please try to follow the recipes closely because the second, third, and fourth Pina Colada must taste like the first. Naturally, the same rule goes for all other cocktails.

Section Four: Again, this section has most of my signature cocktails. These cocktails are designed to give a quick buzz. The preparation of these cocktails is what makes them so exotic and most are for hard core customers. Please follow the recipes as stated because if you're off by even a 1/4 oz. of an ingredient it may not taste the way it should.

As a bartender you won't want to get your customers intoxicated. As they walk through the door keep in mind that you, the bartender, are there to make money, so you will need to regulate the way your customers drink most of the time. Many times a new customer will walk in and ask you to recommend something nice. At this point, you would want to recommend something from section two (2). As your shift progresses you should pay attention to how many drinks the customer has consumed and the effect it has on him before moving to the next level of stronger cocktails. Remember, the more the customer respects you the more comfortable he and will be and be more likely to come back on a regular basis. Being a small island bar you will naturally run out of a certain style of glasses, garnishes or even mixes. As can be seen from the photos in this book any glass will do, as will most garnishes, but you must know how to substitute ingredients.

Kirk Westby's
Belizian Guide of Island Drinks

The following listing of drinks are broken down into four sections:

Virgin Drinks which contain no alcohol

Sneaky Kirk drinks which are so smooth and so very good

Standard Island Drinks these are some of the famous standbys found in bars all over the tropics

Kirk's Signature Cocktails for a Quick Buzz (Island Death). These are the drinks that will put you in the ditch, luckily on this island we don't have any ditches we don't have any cars either.

Virgin Drinks
Designed for
Those that want to remain Virgins

Banana Shake
Chocolate Colada
Chocolate Milk Shake
Cream Soda
Fruit Punch Daiquiri
Grapefruit Daiquiri
Lime Daiquiri
Mango Colada
Mango Daiquiri
Nut Cracker Virgin
Orange Daiquiri
Piña Colada Daiquiri
Pineapple Daiquiri
Shirley Temple
Strawberry Colada
Strawberry Daiquiri
Strawberry Milk Shake

Bartender!! Bartender!!

Virgin Banana Shake

1/2 Banana
1 oz Coconut Cream
A twist of Lime
2 oz Milk

Blend all ingredients together with ice. Serve in a cocktail glass. Garnish with a cherry.

Virgin Chocolate Colada

1 1/2 oz Coconut Cream
3/4 oz Chocolate Syrup
3 oz Pineapple Juice
1 oz Milk
Garnish with a chocolate swirl around the inside of the glass.
Blend all the ingredients together with ice then place in the garnished glass.

Virgin Chocolate Milk Shake

1 1/2 oz Chocolate Syrup
5 oz Milk
1/2 oz Simple Syrup
Blend all ingredients together with ice until slightly frozen. Garnish cocktail glass with a chocolate swirl. Add all blended ingredients in the glass.

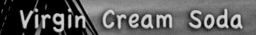

Virgin Cream Soda

8 oz Red Fanta
1 oz Natural Milk
Ice

In a cocktail glass put 4-5
cubes of ice. Fill the glass
with red Fanta top it off
with the natural milk.
Garnish with a cherry.

Virgin Fruit
Punch Daiquiri

1 1/2 oz Fruit Punch
Concentrate
1 1/2 oz Sweetened
Lime Juice
A twist of Lime

Blend all ingredients
together with ice. Serve
in a Daiquiri Glass.
Garnish with a cherry.

Virgin Grapefruit Daiquiri

1 1/2 oz Grapefruit
Juice
1 1/2 oz Sweetened Lime
Juice
A Twist of Lime

Blend all ingredients together
with ice. Serve in a Daiquiri
glass. Garnish with a slice of
Lime or Grapefruit.

Virgin Lime Daiquiri

1 1/2 oz Lime Concentrate
1 1/2 oz Sweetened Lime
Juice
A twist of Lime

Blend all ingredients
together with ice. Serve
in a Daiquiri glass.
Garnish with a slice of
lime.

Virgin Mango Colada

2 oz Mango Juice
1 1/2 oz Coconut Cream
1 1/2 oz Milk
2 drops Grenadine

Blend all the ingredients together with ice. Serve in a cocktail glass. Garnish with 2 drops of Grenadine and a cherry on top.

Virgin Mango Daiquiri

1 1/2 oz Mango Juice
1 1/2 oz Sweetened Lime Juice
A twist of Lime
Blend all the ingredients with ice. Serve in a Daiquiri glass. Garnish with a slice of lime.

Virgin Nut Cracker Daiquiri

1/2 Snickers Candy Bar
3/4 oz Coconut Cream
3 oz Milk
1/2 oz Chocolate Syrup

Blend all ingredients together with ice. Serve in a cocktail glass. Garnish with chocolate syrup and a peanut.

Virgin Orange Daiquiri

1 1/2 oz Orange Juice
1 1/2 oz Sweetened Lime Juice
A twist of Lime

Blend all ingredients together with ice. Serve in a Daiquiri glass. Garnish with a slice Of orange.

Virgin Piña Colada

2 oz Coconut Cream
3 oz Pineapple Juice
1 oz Milk
Few drops Grenadine

Blend all ingredients together with ice. Serve in a cocktail glass. Garnish with 3-5 drops of Grenadine and a cherry on top.

Virgin Pineapple Daiquiri

1 1/2 oz Pineapple Juice
1 1/2 oz Sweetened Lime Juice
A twist of Lime

Blend all ingredients with ice. Serve in a Daiquiri glass. Garnish with a slice of Lime.

Shirley Temple

1/4 oz Grenadine
5 cubes Ice
8 oz Sprite

In a cocktail glass place
5 cubes of ice. Fill glass
with Sprite. Add 1/4 oz
of Grenadine. Stir and
garnish with a cherry.

Virgin Strawberry Colada

1 1/2 oz Coconut Cream
3/4 oz Strawberry Mix
3 oz Pineapple Juice
1 oz Milk

Blend all ingredients together
with ice. Serve in a cocktail
glass. Garnish with 3-5 drops
of Grenadine and a cherry on
top.

Virgin Strawberry Daiquiri

1 1/2 oz Strawberry Mix
1 1/2 oz Sweetened Lime Juice
A twist of lime

Blend all the ingredients together with ice. Serve in a Daiquiri glass. Garnish with a slice of lime.

Virgin Strawberry Milk Shake

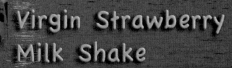

1 1/2 oz Strawberry Mix
4 oz Milk
1/2 oz Sugar

Blend all ingredients together with ice. Serve in a cocktail glass. Garnish with cherry on top.

Sneaky Kirks

Kirk's Signature Cocktails. Designed to hide
the alcohol taste for customer's who
are just starting out

BAILEYS COLADA

BANANA DAIQUIRI

BLUE COSMOPOLITAN

BLUE MARGARITA

BRANDY SOUR SPECIAL

CA COW EXPLOSION

CARIB ALIZAE ORANGE

CARIB ALIZAE
     RASPBERRY

CARIB BANANA COOLER

CARIB MELON COOLER

CARIB PEACH COOLER

CHERRY COOLER

CHOCOLATE ICE

CHOCOLATE MARTINI

CINNAMON BALL

COLA COLADA

COSMOPOLITAN

CREAMY PANTY

DEATH BY CHOCOLATE

EX-VIRGIN

FANTA SHANDY

KAMIKAZE

MANGO DAIQUIRI

MELON BALL

MELON COLADA

NUT CRACKER

OOH KIRK

ORIGINAL SHANDY

PANTY RIPPER

PASSION FRUIT

PIÑA COLADA

PINEAPPLE DAIQUIRI

POP MY CHERRY

RUM PUNCH

SEX-IN-THE-SAND

SKINNY DIP

STRAWBERRY COLADA

STRAWBERRY
MARGARITA

WESTBY ICE

WESTBY PUNCH

WINE COOLER

WOO WOW

A tourist after having a couple of Sneaky Kirk drinks. Eric, the local dive instructor is in the middle. The tip jar, which will be discussed later is in the foreground.

Baileys Colada

1 oz Baileys
1 1/2 oz Coconut Cream
1/2 oz Milk
1/2 oz Dark Rum

Place all ingredients in the blender with ice. Blend and serve in a cocktail glass. Garnish with chocolate syrup on top.

Banana Daiquiri

1/2 Banana
1/2 oz Simple Syrup
or 1 1/2 tsp Sugar
1 1/2 oz Lite Rum
1/2 oz Triple Sec

Place all ingredients in the blender with ice. Blend and serve in a Daiquiri glass. Garnish with a cherry on an umbrella.

Blue Cosmopolitan

1 1/2 oz Vodka
1/4 oz Grand Marnier
2 oz Cranberry Juice
A twist of Lime
1/4 oz Blue Curacao

Shake and strain into a Martini glass. Garnish with a cherry on the rim of the glass.

Blue Margarita

1 1/2 oz Tequila
1/2 oz Triple Sec
A twist of fresh Lime
1/2 oz Sweetened Lime juice
1 oz Blue Curacao

Blend all ingredients with ice. Serve in a Margarita glass. Garnish with Lime rubbed around the glass and place glass in a tray with salt then add ingredients and a slice of Lime.

Brandy Sour Special

1 1/2 oz Brandy
5 oz Lime Juice

Shake with ice and serve in an old fashion glass. Garnish with a slice of Lime.

Ca Cow Explosion

1 Stout
3/4 oz Dark Rum
1/2 oz chocolate syrup

Pour 1 stout in cocktail glass, then in a plastic cup put 3/4 oz dark rum, add 1/2 oz chocolate syrup, mix well!!!! Then pour into 1 1/2 oz shot glass. Drop the shot glass inside the Stout while serving.

Caribbean Alizae Orange

1/2 oz Dark Rum
3/4 oz Peach Schnapps
1/2 oz Vodka
2 oz Orange Juice

Shake all ingredients together with ice. Strain into an old fashion glass. Garnish with a slice of orange.

Caribbean Alizae Raspberry

1/2 oz Dark Rum
3/4 oz Peach Schnapps
1/2 oz Vodka
2 oz Orange Juice

4-6 drops of Grenadine

Shake all ingredients together with ice. Strain into an old fashion glass. Garnish with a slice of orange or lime.

Caribbean Banana Cooler

1 oz Banana Liquor
1/2 oz Vodka
1/2 oz Lite Rum
2 oz Dry White Wine
3 oz Sprite

Place all ingredients in a tall glass and stir with a straw.
Garnish with a cherry on a umbrella.

Caribbean Melon Cooler

1 oz Melon Liquor
1/2 oz Vodka
2 oz Dry White Wine
3 oz Sprite

Place all ingredients in a tall glass and stir with a straw. Garnish with a cherry or an umbrella.

Caribbean Peach Cooler

1 oz Peach Liquor
1/2 oz Vodka
2 oz Dry White Wine
3 oz Sprite

Place all ingredients in a tall glass and stir with a straw. Garnish with a cherry or an umbrella.

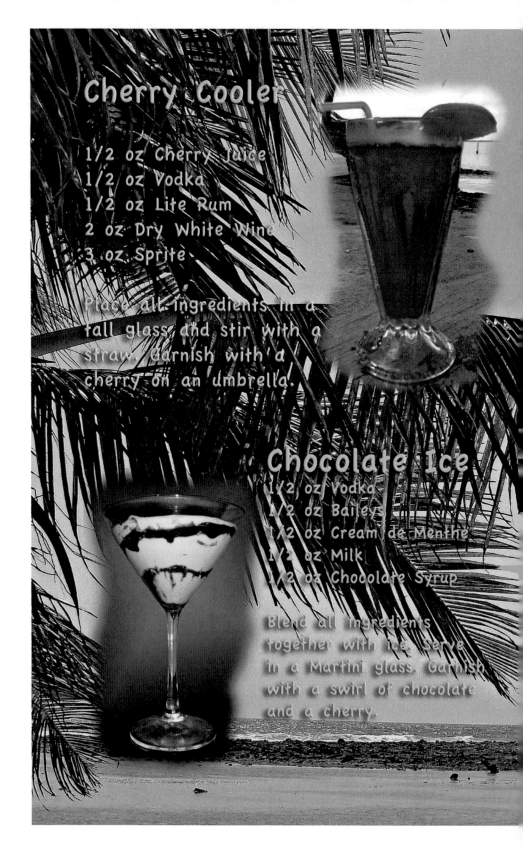

Cherry Cooler

1/2 oz Cherry Juice
1/2 oz Vodka
1/2 oz Lite Rum
2 oz Dry White Wine
3 oz Sprite

Place all ingredients in a
tall glass and stir with a
straw. Garnish with a
cherry on an umbrella.

Chocolate Ice

1/2 oz Vodka
1/2 oz Baileys
1/2 oz Cream de Menthe
1/2 oz Milk
1/2 oz Chocolate Syrup

Blend all ingredients
together with ice. Serve
in a Martini glass. Garnish
with a swirl of chocolate
and a cherry.

Chocolate Martini

1/2 oz Vermouth Dry
1 oz Crème de Cocoa
1/4 oz Chocolate Syrup
1 1/2 oz Vodka

Shake and strain into a
Martini glass. Garnish
with an olive on the side.

Cinnamon Ball

1/2 oz Cinnamon Powder
1/2 oz Nutmeg Powder
1/2 oz Vanilla
4 oz Sugar
1 oz 151 Strong Rum
3 oz Water

For this cocktail a pre-bar mix
may be made to make it easy.
Place the first four ingredients
in the blender, mix until
creamy, then store. Does not
need to be refrigerated.

Cola Colada

1 1/2 oz Coconut Cream
1 1/2 oz Pineapple Juice
1 1/2 oz Dark Rum
1 oz Kahlua
1/2 oz Milk

Place all ingredients in
the blender with ice.
Blend and serve in a
cocktail glass. Garnish
with a cherry on top.

Cosmopolitan

1 1/2 oz Vodka
1/4 oz Grand Marnier
2 oz Cranberry Juice
A twist of lime

Shake and strain into a
Martini glass. Garnish
with a cherry on the
rim of the glass.

Creamy Panty

1 oz Dark Rum
1/2 oz Crème de Cocoa
1/2 oz Anise & Pepper
1 oz Milk

Pour all ingredients on
ice. Serve in an old
fashion glass. Garnish
with a cherry.

Death By Chocolate

1/2 oz Baileys
1/2 oz Kahlua
1/2 oz Dark Rum
1/2 oz Coconut Cream
1/2 oz Milk
1 oz Chocolate Syrup

Blend all ingredients with
ice, serve in a cocktail
glass & garnish with
chocolate on top.

EX Virgin

1 oz Brandy
1/2 oz Dark Rum
1 1/2 oz Coconut Cream
1/2 oz Milk
3-4 drops Grenadine

Blend all ingredients with
ice. Serve in an old fashion
glass. Garnish with nutmeg
powder, 3-4 drops of Grenadine across the top then add
a straw.

Fanta Shandy

4 oz Beer
3 oz Orange Fanta
3-5 Ice Cubes

In a tall glass put the
beer, ice and finish
filling up the glass with
orange fanta, stir with a
straw. Garnish with a
slice of orange.

Mango Daiquiri

2 oz Mango Squash
1 1/2 oz Lite Rum
A twist of fresh Lime

Place all ingredients in the blender with ice. Blend and serve in a Daiquiri glass. Garnish with a slice of Lime.

Melon Ball

1 oz Melon Liquor
1 oz Vodka
3 oz Pineapple Juice

Shake all ingredients together with ice. Strain into an old fashion glass. Garnish with a cherry.

Melon Colada

1 1/2 oz Melon Liquor
1 oz Vodka
1 1/2 oz Pineapple Juice
1 1/2 oz Coconut Cream
1/2 oz Milk

Place all the ingredients in the blender with ice. Blend and serve in a cocktail glass. Garnish with a cherry and a slice of pineapple, lime or an umbrella.

Nut Cracker

1/2 oz Snickers Candy Bar
1/2 oz Amaretto
1/2 oz Vodka
1/2 oz Baileys
1 1/2 oz Coconut Cream
1/2 oz Milk
1 oz Chocolate Syrup

Snickers bar can be substituted with 1 tsp peanut butter or 1 oz fresh peanuts. Blend all ingredients with ice. Serve in a cocktail glass. Garnish with a chocolate swirl and a peanut.

Ooh Kirk

1 oz Coconut Cream
1 oz Baile's
1 oz Dark Rum
1 oz Chocolate Syrup
1/2 oz Milk
1 1/2 Oreo Cookies

Blend all ingredients
together with ice. Serve in a
cocktail glass. Garnish with a
swirl of chocolate and top
with remaining Oreo.

Original Shandy

4 oz Beer
3 oz Sprite
3-5 Ice Cubes

In a tall glass put the
beer, ice and finish
filling up the glass
with Sprite, stir with
a straw. Garnish with
a cherry.

Panty Ripper

1 1/2 oz Coconut Rum
3 oz Pineapple Juice

Place all ingredients in a high ball glass with ice. Stir with a straw. Garnish with a pineapple slice.

Passion Fruit

1/2 oz Vodka
1/2 oz Lite White Rum
1/2 oz Peach Liquor
3-5 Drops of Grenadine
1 oz Cranberry juice
2 oz Sprite

Place all ingredients in a tall glass and stir with a straw. Garnish with a cherry.

Piña Colada

2 oz Dark Rum
2 oz Pineapple Juice
2 oz Coconut Cream
1/2 oz Milk

Place all the ingredients in
the blender with ice. Blend
and serve in a cocktail glass.
Garnish with a cherry and a
slice of pineapple on an
umbrella.

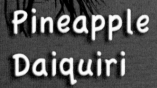

Pineapple
Daiquiri

2 oz Pineapple Squash
1 1/2 oz Lite Rum

Place all ingredients in
the blender with ice.
Blend and serve in a
Daiquiri glass. Garnish
with a slice of lime and a
cherry.

Pop My Cherry

1 oz Brandy
1/2 oz Blue Curacao
1/2 oz Vodka
3-5 Drops Grenadine
2 oz Sprite

Shake all ingredients with ice. Serve in an old fashion glass.

Rum Punch

1 1/2 oz Lite Rum
1 oz Orange Juice
1 oz Pineapple Juice
1 oz Grapefruit Juice
1/4 oz Grenadine

Shake all ingredients together with ice. Serve in a cocktail glass. Garnish with a slice of orange and a cherry on an umbrella.

Sex In The Sand

1/2 oz Lite Rum
1/2 oz Vodka
1/2 oz Peach Liquor
2 oz Orange Juice
1 oz Cranberry Juice
2-3 Drops of Grenadine

Pour all ingredients into a tall
glass with ice, stir with a
straw. Garnish with a cherry.

Skinny Dip

1/2 oz Dark Rum
1 oz Vodka
2 oz Orange Juice
2 oz Grapefruit Juice

Place all ingredients on
ice. Serve in a Margarita
glass. Garnish with a
slice of orange.

Strawberry Colada

2 oz. Dark Rum
2 oz Pineapple Juice
2 oz Coconut Cream
1/2 oz Milk
1 1/2 oz Strawberry Mix

Place all ingredients in the
blender with ice. Blend and serve
in a cocktail glass. Garnish with
a cherry and a slice of pineapple
or an umbrella.

Strawberry
Margarita

1 1/2 oz Tequila
1/2 oz Triple Sec
Twist of fresh Lime
1/2 oz Sweetened Lime juice
1 oz Strawberry Mix

Blend all ingredients with ice.
Serve in a Margarita glass.
Garnish with lime rubbed around
the glass and place glass in a
tray with salt then add ingredients and a slice of lime

Westby Ice

1 oz Vodka
1/4 oz Triple Sec
3/4 oz Sprite
1/4 oz Grapefruit Squash
2-3 Drops of Fresh Lime
Juice

Put all ingredients in a tall
glass slowly fill with Sprite,
stir with a straw. Garnish
with a slice of lime.

Westby Punch

1 oz Lite Rum
1/2 oz Dark Rum
1/2 oz Amaretto
1/2 oz Peach Liquor
1/4 oz Grenadine
1 oz Pineapple Juice
1 oz Grapefruit Juice
1 oz Orange Juice

Blend all ingredients with ice.
Serve in a cocktail glass.
Garnish with a slice of orange.

Wine Cooler

2 oz White Wine
1/2 oz Vodka
5 oz Sprite

Place all ingredients in
a tall glass and stir
with a straw. Garnish
with a cherry or lime.

Woo Wow

1/2 oz Peach Liquor
1/2 oz Vodka
1/2 oz Dark Rum
1/2 oz Cranberry Juice
A twist of fresh lime

Shake all ingredients
together with ice. Serve
in a tall glass. Garnish
with a cherry.

Kirk's Fruit Punches

These are just tasty fruit punches, with a bit of alcohol that are so typical of the drinks made from ingredients commonly found in this part of the world.

Home Style Banana Daiquiri

2 oz dark Rum
2 tsp Sugar
2-3 shakes of Cinnamon
1/2 oz Vanilla
1/2 glass natural milk
2 cups crushed ice
1/2 Banana

Put all ingredients in a blender and blend for 1-2 minutes.

Home Style Papaya Shake

4 oz diced Papaya
2 tsp Sugar
2-3 shakes Nutmeg powder
4 oz Milk
2 oz Dark Rum

Put all ingredients in a blender add 2 cups of crushed ice and blend for 1-2 minutes.

Home Style Pineapple Daiquiri

Dice 4 oz fresh pineapple than add:
2 tsp Sugar
2 oz Vodka
A twist of lime

Place all ingredients in a blender then add 2 cups of crushed ice and blend for 2-3 minutes.

Home Style Mango Daiquiri

Peel 1 medium size ripe Mango, slice off the flesh from the seed. Dice the Mango.
4 tsp sugar
2 oz Dark rum

Put all ingredients in a blender, add 1/4 glass of water 2 cups crushed ice and blend for 2-3 minutes.

Home Style Cantaloupe Shake

4 oz Diced Cantaloupe
2 oz Sugar
2-3 shakes Nutmeg
2 oz of any Dark Rum
3 oz Milk

Put all ingredients in a blender, add 2 cups crushed ice and blend for 2-3 minutes. AHA!!! YOU just made yourself a treat.

Home Style Fruit Punch Shake

4 oz Milk
2 shakes of Cinnamon
3 oz of Dark Rum
2 cups ice
3 Tsp Sugar
1/2 Banana
1/2 Mango
1 section Cantaloupe

Throw all ingredients in blender, add sugar and blend for 2-3 minutes. Makes 3 servings.

Standard Island Cocktails

Amaretto Sour	Mango Memory
Amnesia/Special	Mandingo Colada
Bend Down Baby	Margarita
Bitchin Slap	Orgasm
Bitch-y-Colada	Orange Daiquiri
Bloody Mary	Orange Memory
Blue Boy	Pink Passion
Blue Lagoon	Poor Man Martini
Blue Marlin	Pussy Cave
BZ Colada	Quick Death Shot
Carnal	Refresher
Creole Bulldog	Red Rose Martini
Embryo Shot	Red Snapper Shot
Fire Ants Sting	Salty Dog
Fuzzy Navel	Sand Fire Kamikaze
Golden Pea	Sex Machine
Grapefruit Daiquiri	Sexy Lady
Grapefruit Memory	Skip and Come Naked
Hard Day	Slip Off Your Thong
Jade	Smith & Westby
Jungle Juice	Special Margarita
K. W. J.	Strawberry Daiquiri
Kirk Wall Banger	Tear up Brief
Kirk Westby Collins	Test Tube Shot
Krazy Kool-Aid	To the Moon
Land Slide	Toasted Coca
Lemon Drops	Tranquility
Liquid Cocaine	Under the Sheet
Love Potion	White Russian
Man Command	Weed Cutter

Amaretto Sour

1 1/2 oz Amaretto
3 oz Sweetened Lime
Juice

Pour all ingredients on
ice. Garnish with a
slice of lime.

Amnesia Special

1 1/2 oz Baileys
1 oz Vodka
1 1/2 oz Crème de
Menthe
2 oz Milk

Shake all ingredients
together with ice. Strain
into a Martini glass.
Garnish with a cherry.

Bend Down Baby

1 oz Vodka
1/2 oz Lite Rum
1/2 oz Amaretto
1 1/2 oz Lime Juice

Pour all ingredients on ice.

Bitchin Slap

1 oz Brandy
1/2 oz Triple Sec
2 oz Lime Juice

Pour all ingredients on ice. Serve in a high ball glass. Garnish with a slice of orange.

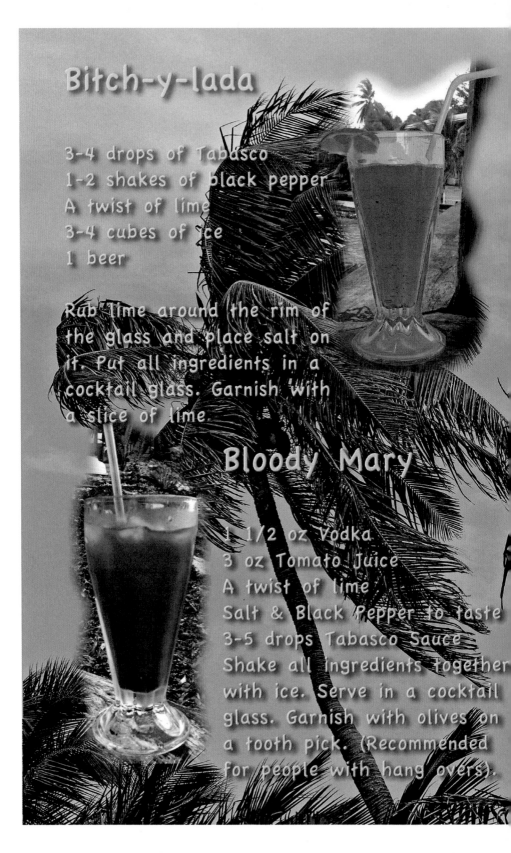

Bitch-y-lada

3-4 drops of Tabasco
1-2 shakes of black pepper
A twist of lime
3-4 cubes of ice
1 beer

Rub lime around the rim of
the glass and place salt on
it. Put all ingredients in a
cocktail glass. Garnish with
a slice of lime.

Bloody Mary

1 1/2 oz Vodka
3 oz Tomato Juice
A twist of lime
Salt & Black Pepper to taste
3-5 drops Tabasco Sauce
Shake all ingredients together
with ice. Serve in a cocktail
glass. Garnish with olives on
a tooth pick. (Recommended
for people with hang overs).

Blue Boy

1/2 oz Blue Curacao
1/2 oz Coconut Rum
1/2 oz Peach Schnapps
1/2 oz sweet Lime Juice
1 oz Sprite
2-3 drops Grenadine

Pour all ingredients in a
cocktail glass with ice.
Garnish with a slice of orange.

Blue Lagoon

1/2 oz Vodka
1 oz Lite Rum
1/2 oz Blue Curacao
3 oz Orange Juice
A Twist of Lime

Pour all ingredients
on ice.

Blue Marlin

1 oz Lite Rum
1/2 oz Blue Curacao
1 oz Lime Juice
1 oz Sprite

Shake with ice and serve in a Martini glass. Garnish with a cherry.

Belize Colada

1/2 oz Coconut Rum
1 oz Dark Rum
2 oz Pineapple Juice
2 oz Coco Lopez
1/2 oz Milk

Blend all ingredients with ice. Serve in a cocktail glass. Garnish with a few drops of Grenadine and two cherries on top.

Carnal

2 oz Lite Rum
3 oz Grapefruit Juice
A twist of lime
3-4 shakes of salt
2 oz water

Shake with ice and serve
in a cocktail glass.

Creole Bulldog

1/2 oz Tia Maria
1/2 oz Vodka
1/2 oz Lite Rum
2 oz Milk
2 oz Coke

Blend all ingredients with
ice. Serve in a cocktail
glass. Garnish with a
cherry on top.

Embryo Shot

1 oz Kahlua
1/2 oz Vodka
2-3 Drops of Baileys

Place Kahlua into a 1 1/2 oz shot glass. Float Vodka on top. Take a long straw and place it inside the Baileys bottle. Cover the top of the straw with 1 finger and remove the straw then place it in the middle of the shot, add 2-3 drops of Baileys in the middle creating an embryo.

Fire Ants Sting

1/2 oz Vodka
1/2 oz Gin
Juice from 1/2 lime
1 oz Sweetened Lime Juice
2 oz Soda Water

Shake all ingredients with ice and serve.

Fuzzy Navel

1 oz Peach Schnapps
1/2 oz Vodka
3 oz Orange Juice

Shake and pour on ice.
Garnish with a cherry or
fruit on the glass.

Golden Pea

1/2 oz Goldschlager
1/4 oz Southern Comfort
1/4 oz Amaretto
1/2 oz Triple Sec

Shake all ingredients
together with ice. Strain
into a Martini glass.

Grapefruit Daiquiri

2 oz Grapefruit Juice
1 1/2 oz Lite Rum
A twist of Lime

Blend all ingredients with ice. Serve in a Daiquiri glass. Garnish with a slice of Grape-fruit.

Grapefruit Memory

1/2 oz Vodka
1 oz Lite Rum
3 oz Grapefruit Juice
2-3 shakes Black Pepper
2-3 shakes of salt

Shake with ice and serve in an old fashion glass. Garnish with a slice of lime.

Hard Day

1 oz Dry White Wine
1 oz Vodka
1/2 oz Amaretto
2 oz Sweetened Lime
Juice

On ice, garnish with a
slice of Lime.

Jade

1 1/2 oz Life Rum
1/2 oz Crème de
Menthe
1/2 oz Triple Sec

Shake all ingredients
with ice. Strain into
2 shot glasses.

Jungle Juice

1 oz Vodka
1 oz Dark Rum
1/2 oz Triple Sec
1 oz Lime Juice
1 oz Cranberry Juice
1 oz Orange Juice
1 oz Pineapple Juice

Shake all ingredients with ice. Serve in a cocktail glass.

K.W.J.

1/2 oz Anise and Pepper
1 oz Campari
1 1/2 oz Red Bull
1 1/2 oz Cranberry Juice
1/2 oz Bitters

Shake all ingredients together with ice.

Kirk Wall Banger

1/2 oz Lite Rum
1 oz Vodka
4 oz Orange Juice
1/4 oz Galliano
2-3 drops Grenadine

Put all ingredients in a glass
filled with ice. Float 1/4 oz
Galliano. Garnish with a slice
of pineapple and a cherry on
a tooth pick and 2-3 drops of
Grenadine on top of the
Galliano.

Kirk Westby Collins

1 oz Gin
1/2 oz Lite Rum
2 oz Soda Water
1 oz Sweetened Lime
Juice

Pour all ingredients
on ice. Garnish with
a slice of orange.

Krazy Cool Aid

1 oz Amaretto
1 oz Southern Comfort
1 oz Dark Rum
1 oz Sweetened Lime
Juice
3 oz Cranberry Juice

Shake all ingredients
together. Pour into a
cocktail glass. Garnish
with a cherry, a slice of
lime and an umbrella.

Land Slide

1/2 oz Vodka
1 oz Kahlua
1/2 oz Baileys
1/3 oz Coconut Cream

Blend all ingredients
except Kahlua with ice.
Add Kahlua in a
cocktail glass then all
blended ingredients.
Garnish with a cherry.

Lemon Drops

1 oz Vodka
1 slice of lime
with Sugar

Serve in the same
order as tequila.

Liquid Cocaine

1 oz Coconut Rum
1 oz Crème de Cocoa
dark
1 oz Milk

Shake all ingredients
together with ice. Strain
into 3 shot glasses.

Love Potion

1 1/2 oz Southern
Comfort
1 oz Dark Rum
1/2 oz Grenadine
2 oz Milk

Shake all ingredients
together with ice. Strain

Man Command

1/2 oz Lite Rum
1/2 oz Vermouth
1 oz Whiskey

Place all ingredients
in glass with ice and
stir.

Mango Memory

1/2 oz Vodka
1 oz Lite Rum
3 oz Mango Juice
2-3 shakes Black Pepper
2-3 shakes of salt

Shake with ice and serve
in an old fashion glass.
Garnish with a slice of
lime.

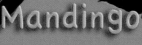

Mandingo
Colada

2 oz Crushed Peanuts or
1 Munch bar
2 oz Coconut Cream
1 1/2 oz Vodka
3 oz Milk

Blend all ingredients with
ice. Serve in a cocktail
glass. Garnish with a
cherry.

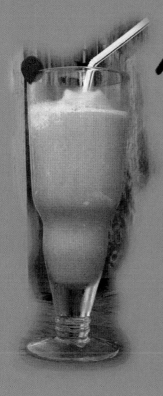

Margarita

1 1/2 oz Tequila
1/2 oz Triple Sec
Juice from 1/2 a Lime
1 oz Sweetened Lime Juice

Blend all ingredients together with ice. Salt and lime on the rim of the glass. Garnish with a slice of lime.

Orange Daiquiri

2 oz Orange Concentrate
1 1/2 oz Lite Rum
A twist of Lime

Blend all ingredients with ice. Serve in a Daiquiri glass. Garnish with a slice of orange.

Orange Memory

1/2 oz Vodka
1 oz Lite Rum
3 oz Orange Juice
1 Dash of Hot Sauce
2-3 shakes Black Pepper
2-3 shakes of salt

Recommended as a
refreshing drink.

Orgasm

1/2 oz Kahlua
1/2 oz Baileys
1/2 oz Brandy
2 oz Milk

Shake all ingredients
with ice. Pour into an
old fashion glass.

Pink Passion

1 1/2 oz Vodka
3 oz Grapefruit
Juice
3-5 drops Grenadine

Shake all ingredients
together with ice.
Serve in a Martini
glass. Garnish with
a slice of orange.

Poor Man
Martini

1 1/2 oz Vodka
1/2 oz Dry Red Wine
1/2 oz Vermouth Dry

Shake all ingredients
together with ice. Strain
into a Martini glass.
Garnish with an olive.

Pussy Cave

1/2 oz Green Crème de Menthe
1/2 oz float Galliano
1/2 oz float Brandy
2 drops Grenadine

Put all ingredients into a 1 1/2 oz shot glass. Top off with 2 drops of Grenadine.

Quick Death Shot

1/2 oz Baileys
1/2 oz Kahlua
1/4 oz Midori Melon

In a 1 1/2 oz shot glass float all ingredients in order of Kahlua at the bottom, Baileys next, top off with Midori Melon.

Red Rose Martini

1 1/2 oz Vodka
1/2 oz Dry Vermouth
1 oz Dry Red Wine

Shake all ingredients together with ice. Strain into a Martini glass. Garnish with a slice of lime.

Red Snapper Shot

1 oz Amaretto
1 oz Crown Royal
2 oz Cranberry Juice

Shake ingredients together with ice. Strain into 2 shot glasses.

Refresher

1 1/2 oz Vodka
2 oz Soda Water
1 oz Cranberry Juice
A Twist of Lime

Pour all ingredients on ice. Garnish with a slice of lime.

Salty Dog

1 1/2 oz Vodka
4 oz Grapefruit Juice

Take a slice of lime and rub around the rim of the glass. Turn glass upside down and dip into a tray of salt. Add ice and ingredients in the glass. Garnish with a slice of lime.

Sand Fire Kamikaze

2 oz Vodka
1/2 oz Triple Sec
1/2 oz Fresh Lime Juice
1/4 oz Blue Curacao
1 1/2 oz Lite Rum
2 oz Sweetened Lime juice

Shake all ingredients together. Strain into 6 shot glasses. A Kirk signature cocktail for a Quick Buzz.

Sex Machine

1 oz Grand Marnier
1/2 oz Lite Rum
1 oz Vodka
2-3 drops Grenadine
3 oz Cranberry Juice

Serve in a high ball glass with ice.

Sexy Lady

1 oz Amaretto
1/2 oz Crème de Cocoa
Brown
1 oz Dark Rum
1 oz Milk

Shake all ingredients
with ice.

Skip & Come Naked

1 oz Gin
2 oz Lime Juice
3 oz Beer
1/2 oz Vodka

In a cocktail glass
add ice then all the
ingredients.

Slip Off The Thong

1/2 oz Amaretto
1/2 oz Apple Schnapps
1/2 oz Raspberry Schnapps
1/2 oz Lite Rum

Pour all ingredients on ice. Garnish with a slice of orange.

Smith & Westby

1 oz Southern Comfort
1 oz White Rum

Pour all ingredients on ice. Garnish with a cherry.

Special Margarita

1 oz Tequila
1/2 oz Triple Sec
1/2 oz Cointreau
1 oz Sweetened Lime Juice
Juice from 1/2 Lime

Blend all ingredients. Put lime juice and salt on the rim of the glass. Garnish with a slice of lime.

Strawberry Daiquiri

2 oz Strawberry Mix
1 1/2 oz Lite Rum
A twist of lime.

Blend all ingredients with ice. Serve in a Daiquiri glass. Garnish with a slice of lime.

Tear Up
Brief

1 1/2 oz Coconut Rum
4 oz Grapefruit Juice

Pour all ingredients on
ice. Garnish with a
cherry.

Test Tube
Shot

1 oz Coconut Rum
1 oz Blue Curacao
1 oz Lite Rum

Pour Ingredients in a
test tube. Shake 2 oz
beer on top and let
foam up and serve.

To The Moon

1/2 oz Kahlua
1/2 oz Galliano
1/2 oz Melon Liquor
1/2 oz Lite Rum

Shake all ingredients
with ice

Toasted Coca

1 oz Baileys
1/2 oz Brandy
1/2 oz Amaretto
2 oz Milk

Blend all ingredients
together with ice
top it off with whip
cream and a cherry.

Tranquility

1 1/2 oz Peach Schnapps
1/2 oz Banana liquor
1/2 oz Gold rum
1/2 oz Lite rum
1 oz Pineapple juice

Shake and strain into an
old fashion glass. Garnish
with two mint leaves and
a cherry.

Under the Sheets

1/2 oz Vodka
1 oz Brandy
1/2 oz Triple Sec
1 oz Lime Juice

Shake ingredients together
with ice. Strain into 3 shot
glasses.

Weed Cutter

1/2 oz Baileys
1/2 oz Cream de Cocoa
1/2 oz Amaretto
1/2 oz Dark Rum
1 oz Milk

Blend all ingredients
together with ice. Serve
in a cocktail glass.

White Russian

1 oz Vodka
1 oz Kahlua
2 oz Milk

Pour all ingredients
on ice.

Kirk's Signature Cocktails
for a Quick Buzz
(Island Death)

Above the Law {shot}

Baby Blow

Banana Hammock

Belizean Ice Tea

Belizean Mama

Belizean Sunset

Belizean Twister

Blue Ice Tea

Caribbean Car Bom

Caribbean Hurricane

Caribbean Zombie

Cherry Bom Shot

Diana Westby Obsession

Earthquake

Fouled Anchor

Hurricane Kirk

Hurricane Tongue

Independence Day Margarita

Kirk's Concussion

Kirk's Motivation

Kirk's Fire Ball Shot

Kirk's Slam Dunk

Leg Spreaders

Mai Tai

Martini Dry Gin

Martini Sweet Gin

Martini Sweet Vodka

Pain Killer

Purple Willie

Red Devil Kamikaze

Screaming Baby

Shania Westby

Slow Screw

Strawberry Rum Sou

Sweet Belizean Bree:

3 Wise Men

Above the Law
{Shot}

In a 1 1/2 oz shot glass
1/2 oz Kahlua
1/4 oz Baileys
1/2 oz 151 Over proof rum
2-3 drops Grenadine

In a 1 1/2 oz shot glass put
1/2 oz Kahlua, float 1/4 oz
Baileys on top of the Kahlua.
Put 1/2 oz 151 strong rum in
a disposable cup add 3-4 drops
of Grenadine into the 151 mix
and float in top of the Baileys
garnished with flames.

Baby Blow

1/2 oz Amaretto
1/2 oz Baileys
1/2 oz Kahlua
1/2 oz Brandy
2 oz Milk

Shake all ingredients with
ice then pour in an old
fashion glass. Garnish with
whip cream and 2 cherries.

Banana Hammock {shot}

1/4 oz Gin
1/2 oz Lite Rum
1/4 oz Amaretto
1/2 oz Vodka
1/2 oz Southern Comfort

Shake with ice and pour into shot glasses.

Belizean Ice Tea

1/2 oz Vodka
1/2 oz Gin
1/2 oz Tequila
1/2 oz Lite Rum
1/2 oz Bacardi
A squeeze of fresh lime

Shake all ingredients with ice, serve in a cocktail glass top off with coke.

Belizean Mama

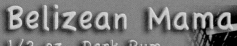

1/2 oz   Dark Rum
1/2 oz Coconut Rum
1/2 oz 151 Over Proof Rum
3/4 oz Kahlua
3 oz Sweetened Lime Juice
A twist of Lime

Shake and pour into and old
fashion glass. Garnish with
a slice of lime.

Belizean Sunset

1 1/2 oz Lite Rum
4 oz Sweetened Lime Juice
A Twist of fresh Lime
1/2 oz Over Proof Rum
1/4 oz Grenadine

Mix first three ingredients
with ice. Put 1/2 oz 151
over proof rum into a plastic
cup add 1/4 oz Grenadine
mix, then float on top,
Garnish with a lime.

Belizean Twister

1 oz Dark Rum
1 oz 151 Strong Rum
1 oz Orange Juice
1/2 oz Lime Juice
1/2 oz Grapefruit Juice

Blend with ice, serve in a cocktail glass. Garnish with a slice of lime and orange.

Blue Ice Tea

1/2 oz Vodka
1/2 oz Gin
1/2 oz Tequila
1/2 oz Lite Rum
1/2 oz Blue Curacao

Shake all ingredients with ice, serve in a cocktail glass top off with 3 oz sprite and garnish with a slice of lime.

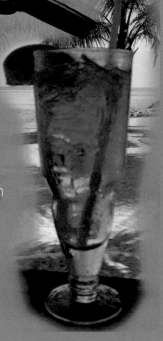

Caribbean Car Bom

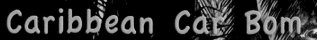

1 Belikin Stout
1 oz Baileys
1/2 oz 151 Over Proof Rum
2-3 drops of Grenadine

Pour a Belikin Stout in a cocktail glass then in a 1 oz shot glass add 3/4 oz Baileys, float 1/4 oz 151 rum on top of the Baileys, add 2-3 drops Grenadine, add flame then drop flaming shot into the Stout. Customer must drink immediately.

Caribbean Hurricane

4 oz Coconut water
1 oz Dark Rum
1/2 oz Lite Rum
1/2 oz Coconut Rum

Pour all ingredients on ice stir with a straw. Garnish with a cherry.

Caribbean Zombie

1/2 oz Brandy
1/2 oz Lite Rum
1/2 oz Dark Rum
1 oz 151 Over Proof Rum
1/2 oz Lime Juice
1/2 oz Pineapple Juice
1/2 Orange Juice
3-5 drops Grenadine

Shake all ingredients with ice and pour into a cocktail glass. Garnish with a slice of pineapple.

Cherry Bom {shot}

2 oz 151 Over Proof Rum
3 oz Cherry Juice

Shake with ice and strain into 6 shot glasses.

Diana Westby Obsession

1/4 oz Gin
1/2 oz Lite Rum
1/4 oz Amaretto
1/2 oz Vodka
1/2 oz Southern Comfort
1/4 oz Banana Liquor
3 oz Pineapple Juice

Shake with ice and put in a cocktail glass.

Earthquake

1/2 oz Vodka
1/2 oz Gin
1/2 oz Tequila
1/2 oz Lemon Rum
3 oz Grapefruit Juice

Shake all ingredients with ice. Pour into a cocktail glass. Top it off with 3 oz Coke. Garnish with a slice of Grapefruit.

Fouled Anchor

1/2 oz Black Label Scotch
1/2 oz Jim Beam
1/2 oz Baileys
1/2 oz Kahlua
1/2 oz Lite Rum
2 oz Milk

Shake ingredients in an old fashion glass.

Hurricane Kirk

1/2 oz Lite Rum
1/2 oz Gin
1/2 oz 151 proof Rum
1/2 oz Bacardi Rum
1/2 oz Tequila
4 oz Orange juice

Shake all ingredients with ice pour in a cocktail glass. Garnish with a slice of orange.

Hurricane Tongue

1/2 oz Coconut Rum
1/4 oz Melon liquor
1/4 oz Triple Sec
1/2 oz Amaretto
1/2 oz Gold Rum
2 oz Orange juice
Pour all ingredients over ice
in a cocktail glass garnish
with a slice of Lime and a
straw then float 1 oz. Cranberry on top.

Independence Day Margarita

2 oz Tequila
1 oz Triple Sec
Zest of 1 Lime
2 oz sweet Lime juice
Blend with ice
Pour into 3 plastic cups:
cup #1 add 3/4 oz of
Strawberry mix, Cup #2
add 1/2 oz blue Curaçao,
cup #3 plain. Assemble as
in photo to form the
Belizean flag.

Kirk's Concussion

1/2 oz Kahlua
1/2 oz Baileys
1/2 oz Goldschlager
1/2 oz Lite Rum

Shake all ingredients with ice. Pour in an old fashion glass.

Kirk's Motivation

1/2 oz Goldschlager
1/2 oz Vodka
1/4 oz Blue Curacao
1/2 oz Drambuie
1/2 oz 151 proof Rum
Put all ingredients in a Martini glass and float 1/2 oz 151 strong Rum on top and light it. Then ask your customer to place straw through the flames and drink immediately before the straw melts.

Kirk's Fire Ball

Put 1 ice cold beer in a cocktail glass.
Fill 1 1/2 oz shot glass with 151 strong Rum.

Add flame to the 1 1/2 oz shot glass, hold over the cocktail glass with the beer. Drop the flaming shot inside the cocktail glass, customer must be ready to drink immediately. This drink should work within 10 minutes. Normally 1 is enough and it is not recommended for females. This shot is very effective, the yeast in the beer appears to take the alcohol straight to the brain. There is a 90% chance that the customer will be passed out within 5-10 minutes. Beware!

Kirk's Slam Dunk

1/2 oz Amaretto
1/2 oz Southern Comfort
1/2 oz Gin
1/2 oz Dark Rum
3 oz Sweetened Lime Juice

Shake with ice and pour into a cocktail glass. Garnish with a slice of Lime.

Leg Spreaders

1/2 oz Vodka
1/2 oz Gin
1 oz Lite Rum
1/2 oz 151 Strong Rum
2 oz Orange Juice
2 oz Lime Juice

Shake with ice, serve in a cocktail glass. Garnish with a slice of lime or orange.

Martini Dry Gin

1 1/2 oz Gin
1 1/2 oz Dry Vermouth

Shake with ice and strain
into a Martini glass. Garnish
with a cherry and lemon rind
twist.

Martini Sweet Gin

1 1/2 oz Gin
1 oz Sweet Vermouth

Shake with ice and
strain into a Martini
glass. Garnish with a
cherry and lemon rind
twist.

Martini
Sweet Vodka

1 1/2 oz Vodka
1 oz Sweet Vermouth

Shake with ice and strain into a Martini glass. Garnish with a cherry and lemon rind twist.

Mai Tai

3/4 oz 151 Strong Rum
1/2 oz Lite Rum
3 oz Orange Juice
2 oz Sweetened Lime Juice
1/2 oz Myers Dark Rum

Pour all ingredients on ice in a cocktail glass, stir with a straw. Garnish with a slice of orange then float with 1/2 oz Myers Dark Rum on top.

Pain Killer

1 1/2 oz 151 Strong
Rum
2 oz Orange Concentrate
1/2 oz Triple Sec

Blend all ingredients with
ice. Serve in a cocktail
glass. Garnish with a
slice of orange.

Purple Willie

1 oz Vodka
1/2 oz 151 Over Proof
Rum
3 oz Grape Juice
3-5 Drops Grenadine

Shake with ice and strain
into 5 shot glasses.

Red Devil Kamikaze

1 oz Vodka
3/4 oz 151 Strong Rum
1/2 oz Fresh Lime Juice
1/4 oz Grenadine
2 oz Sweet Lime Juice

Shake all ingredients with ice and strain into 6 shot glasses.

Screaming Baby

1 oz Baileys
1/2 oz Kahlua
1/2 oz Brandy
2 oz Milk
1/2 oz 151 Over proof rum
Pour all ingredients in a Martini glass and float 1/2 oz over proof rum on top. add flames, then the customer must place a straw through the flames and drink before the straw melts.

Shania Westby

1 1/2 oz Coconut Rum
1/2 oz Sweetened Lime juice
3 oz Cranberry Juice
Served in a tall glass on ice garnished with a slice of Lime.

Slow Screw

1/2 oz Gin
1/2 oz Vodka
1/2 oz Southern Comfort
1/2 oz Galliano
3 oz Orange Juice

Shake with ice and pour into a cocktail glass. Garnish with a slice of orange.

Strawberry Rum Sour

1 1/2 oz Lite Rum
1/2 oz Strawberry mix
3 oz Sweetened Lime juice
1 twist of fresh Lemon

Shake all ingredients and
pour into an eight oz
cocktail glass. Garnish with
a slice of Lime.

Sweet Belizean Breeze

1 oz Vodka
1/2 oz 151 Strong Rum
2 oz Cranberry Juice
1 oz Grapefruit Juice

Pour all ingredients on
ice. Garnish with a
cherry.

3 Wise Men

1/2 oz Jim Beam
1/2 oz Jack Daniels
1/2 oz Jose Cuervo
3 oz Sprite

Pour all ingredients on ice.
Garnish with a slice of
lime.

Kirk on Being a Bartender

I have been a bartender in several different locations during my career and for the last few years, have been really lucky to be the bartender at Tobacco Caye Lodge. This is a whole different situation than most bars, and I love it! My bar is a one-person, bare-foot operation.

Over the years I have found a lot of tips and techniques I learned, often the hard way, to be a professional bartender. The following pages contain some of the tips, lessons and rules that I would like to share with potential bartenders.

To be a bartender you must have excellent P.R. (Public Relation) skills. P.R. means being nice to everyone who walks into the bar—be courteous, polite and pay attention to the customer. For example: when taking an order you must say "good morning … how are you doing today?" "May I please take your order? OK I'll be right back with your order." When receiving payments for the order say "thank you—I'll be right back with your change," and when returning with change say "thank you and enjoy your drink." Whenever a new customer walks in or is leaving always bid them the time of day—good morning, good afternoon, or good evening.

You must always remember that you are often dealing with partially intoxicated people. A bartender is not different from anyone else. In a bar dealing with intoxicated people they will sometimes say something aggravating, and you will get upset. All you need to do is just ignore that comment and get on with your job. For example: arguing a point with an intoxicated customer can easily be resolved by just ignoring that customer and go attend to another customer who is waiting for your service and saying to the other customer "Hi, may I please take your order." Without showing that person that you might be angry. Never let your customer see that you are angry. When you get angry just take a break, take a deep breath and move on to the next customer. Never make a scene because that same irritating customer might later return to your bar. When this happens just be polite because your job is at stake. Always remember it only takes one person to get out of control and if someone tries to mislead you in any way while on your job don't get upset or you will lose control of your bar, if serious, just inform the security guard and let him handle the situation. For example: if someone owes you money for drinks and doesn't want to pay inform security so he can take care of it and you, the bartender, will be able to focus on the other customers you have to attend to and stay in control.

Hard at Work

Often, when a bartender goes on the job training and walks into an active bar for the first time and sees more people than he could serve at the same time there's a tendency to freeze. This means that you stop and your mind goes blank and you don't know what to do next. My personal advice on how not to freeze while working and to become a successful bartender is that you need to love music. Music is the first form of staying calm. For example: the more people you see around the bar the more nervous you get. At this point you will need to rely on the music to keep you calm. Still nervous? Turn up the music a little bit but not too loud; while turning it up you will also still need to pay keen attention to your customers and their orders.

You don't want to have the music too loud and make your customers feel uncomfortable. You will want to pick a specific spot in the bar where you hear the music most which should help to keep you relaxed. You the bartender, will still be in control of your surroundings. Since you found a spot where you are comfortable you will still need to be able to see each of your customers around your bar. When you see a customer wanting to place an order, fill it, and take the order to them, then go back to your comfort zone. By doing this you will find yourself stepping out of your comfort zone more, often within 2-3 days on the job and interacting more with your customers. You will find that the same customers will keep coming into the bar on a regular basis and having the same drinks over and over again. By this time you should be developing a hand signal technique with your regulars. An example would be that you can be anywhere in the bar and one of your regulars can raise his hand, glass or bottle and you will know exactly what that customer wants.

You will find that this saves you time as well as less walking around and the customers will look on you as a professional, in tune with them and that you're relaxed and in control in your surroundings. You will also need to pay attention to how your customers around the bar are drinking. This is for your eyes. Every customer with a glass that is half empty should be checked for a refill. You can tell if customers with bottles need a refill based on how far they tilt the bottle back to take a drink. Remember no matter how many times a person may order the same drink always start another drink with a clean glass. Using a fresh glass shows that you are a professional at your job. However, there are times a customer will ask you to use the same glass. Don't forget the previous rule to stay organized, prepare yourself and your bar.

Within 2-3 months on the job your ears should already be adjusted to the sound, so no matter how hard the music is playing you will be able to hear a person placing an order without seeing the customer or knowing their location, you will just be naturally aware of their request and location.

Small drinks are beer, stout, rum, coke, gin, tonic, whiskey, sodas and juice, or any other popular selling drinks in your bar. When you take an order and have turned away you should be tuned in enough to hear any addition to it without turning back and asking the customer to repeat it.

Pay attention to your customers, always listen and respond, be courteous, be friendly, be good at your profession.

Checking Your Money

When working in a bar the light is usually dim making it hard for you to check the currency to see if it's good or not. If you suspect something is wrong my personal advice is quickly dip you finger in water and rub the money 3-5 times, if it is fake there is a 50% chance that the money will shed ink. Keep in mind that a bar is the best place to pass counterfeit currency. If you find out that currency is counterfeit take it to the security personnel so they can deal with it and you won't have to pay for what you just served. Remember stay in control of your bar!

When collecting money from a customer remember that the lights are always dim, try to keep your eyes on the money while it still is in the customers hand until it reaches yours, that way you can have a good look at what you are getting.

You don't want to reach the cashier or cash register and find out that what the customer gave you was not enough to cover the cost of the bill. If that happens then the customer may argue and say that they gave you more than what you got. Mistakes happen all the time, try to stay a step ahead of the game which will make things easier for you and you will again be in control of your surroundings.

When returning change to a costumer make sure the change is in an organized way for easy counting so that when you hand it over to the customer they can make a quick count. While the customer is counting their change don't walk away or turn your back until they have successfully checked and are satisfied. This is to ensure that no confusion occurs because you do not want to be the one loosing any money. By following these steps it will show that you are a professional at you job.

Customers With Caps

On a busy night pay close attention to customers wearing caps. On occasion a customer with a cap places an order and when you serve the order he immediately places a second order. When you walk away to fill the second order he removes his cap, by the time you get back with that order there is a 50% chance you won't recognize that customer again. To avoid this potential problem try collecting for one order at a time.

Who Orders Pays

My personal rule of being a bartender is whoever places the order will pay for that order. This simply means that if someone comes to order a beer from you, then comes and says that my friend over there will pay for it, the only way this will work is if the person who you say will pay gives some kind of signal indicating that it is OK. Same rule goes for someone who is running a tab.

A Few Moves

No matter which bar you work for you will be on your feet a lot, which at some point will affect your back. To ease your aching feet and back I have designed some steps. At this point music is a part of your work life, so these steps should be easy. Try not to lift your feet too high off the ground, moving forward and backwards, make a complete turn on your heels using your body weight. Try not to wear shoes with heels. You will find yourself doing these "dance steps" to the music a lot and you will find yourself less tired at the end of your shift.

Be Organized

The most important thing in a bar is to be prepared and organized. Know where everything is located in your bar so you don't have to be looking for things and wasting time and when you're finished with them put them back in their proper place. Always be prepared for a crowd no matter what; this way you will always be one step ahead of the game. Being one step ahead means you will always be in control.

Knowing how much liquor to put in 1 oz shot glass without using a shot glass

This will only work by using the cadence of your voice, each person has to do their own count. Take a shot glass and pick up a bottle that has a manufacturer's jigger on top, most of our local rum bottles have one. Hold the jigger in front of you and start counting: one thousand, one; one thousand, two; one thousand, three; one thousand, etc., until the glass is fill. When the glass is filled you will have your number, you will no longer need a shot glass.

So when a customer orders a glass of rum and coke, for instance, you simply put ice in the glass pick up the bottle of rum and pour while counting to your number, add coke and serve. When making other cocktails that take multiple types of alcohol in different portions simply divide your count into four. When making a frozen cocktail that has added ingredients like a Piña Colada that has pineapple juice and coconut cream, you can always rely on the cup that is built into the blender cover, it holds 2 oz, so you will know that 1 oz is half full and count backwards for lesser amounts. Please remember to garnish your cocktails, presentation always compliments the taste. I have made recomendations for what to use, but, as you can see from photos in this book there is no hard and fast rule as far as the garnish goes. As a bartender never let a customer walk away from the bar empty handed because you don't have what they want, if you don't have it be sure to always recommend the next best thing. Enjoy your work at all times.

Dealing with Hard Customers

On your busiest nights you, naturally, will find you will be dealing with the hardest of all customers. One may break through the crowd and need serious advice on some personal problem. You, as the bartender, are the best person to talk to. Use the same methods that you learned to control your anger and still be polite without making a scene. At this point it's not only a job so you will need to stop and think about the best answer to give to the customer that would help them with their problem. The end result may make you feel pretty good about yourself. Drinking is not just for fun, people drink for all sorts of reasons and, over time, you will be able to spot these problems in your customers as they approach the bar.

There are always some customers
that will complain.

Tricks of the Trade

Lights—the reason you should always keep the lights dim in
the bar is because people enjoying their drinks don't like
bright lights. The more alcohol they consume the dimmer
they want it. Keeping the lights low will help you to keep
your customers at the bar for longer periods.

You have a full house and nobody is drinking? This means
you're not making any money. A solution for this problem
that often works is to play good dance music and adjust the
air conditioning so it will be a bit warmer; your customers
will be hot and thirsty after working up a sweat on the
dance floor. After 30-45 minutes play relaxing music and by
this time the bar should be swinging and settling back to
normal.

As a bartender you will need to know how to keep yourself
awake throughout your shift. During the first week or two
of work you may find yourself becoming very sleepy at
times. I have found a half of a cigarette will keep me
awake for four to five hours; a cup of coffee will keep me
awake for up to six to eight hours. To each his own and
you will need to find what works for you. You will need to
regulate it carefully because you don't want to get home
and can't sleep.

End of the day and dog tired!

Keep it Clean

At this point you should have already learned to prepare your bar and how to be ready for a crowd at all times. You have learned to put things back in their proper place as you work, now you will need to train yourself to clean as you work. So as you move around the bar taking orders and serving at the same time you will be putting garbage in its proper place and cleaning little things around you. Over time this will happen automatically without you even knowing it. At the end of your busiest shift you will find your bar clean and you can just leave.

Music

One customer can't make changes in your bar's music! There's just one stereo and you can't please everybody by changing the music frequently. Most of the time you're playing for yourself, so you can feel comfortable in your bar. If there are fifteen people in your bar it should take at least four customer requests to change the music style before you do so!

In most small bars the bartender is responsible for the music. My personal advice on how to categorize your music from start to finish is first, you do not want to out play for your customers. Notice how your customers are drinking. The more they are drinking, they will usually want to hear faster and louder music. Say you are at the bar playing "roots reggae" (e.g. Bob Marley) as the evening progresses you would want to switch to "reggae souls." Your next step would be soft dance hall music. Keep paying attention to the type of people you have in your bar! Keep picking up the pace of the music, by monitoring how much alcohol they consume. Try to keep the music in a category selection at all times.

Drinking on the Job

The "how," "why," and "when" to drink on the job. Most establishments don't allow drinking on the job period! My advice: you may need to take a small shot or drink now and again. For instance, the more people at the bar, sometimes can tend to make you nervous, a drink would help to keep you in "control" And again, if you don't want to be the "logy" person in the house a drink will keep you one step behind your customers and keep you in a good mood as well. You're not doing this to get drunk, never, never, never, never, never do that!! Remember you are on the job, drink courteously and cautiously.

How to Stock Up Your Bar Cooler

This system, shown on the next page, will prevent the beer bottles from falling down in your cooler. For instance, you can stock five cases of beer with the caps facing the side walls. One on top of each other one side, and on the other side you can stack five cases of stout facing the other direction. That will leave the middle, optional for Guiness and light beer. You can also pack two cases of each with the cap facing the back of the stout or beer.

Inside a Well Packed Cooler

Tips

In most bars, the bartender has a tip jar. Most people leave or give a tip because of the service you provide, by making them comfortable and serving good cocktails. The better bartender you become, the better tips you make.

The jar is usually placed on top of the bar and it's not something you should be worried about. It will, and should be respected by all customers, because the money that goes in there is not what you worked for, but it is a compliment to your being good at your job.

As you become a better bartender you will find that most of the time your tips will exceed your salary. At most upscale hotels or resorts there is a service charge, it is something like a tip for the service you provide, but that is shared between all the staff for the service provided. It is not like a personal tip, a personal tip means you know what you're doing, and is a way for a customer of saying thanks and that they appreciate your efforts.

Always try to keep your customer happy, satisfied and having fun. Most of the time it's not about making the best drinks, but being nice, friendly and respectful under all conditions and this will make you a good bartender. By doing this, it explains that it is my tip jar and everything will flow from there.

Customers that Have Had Too Much

Most people tend to bar hop from one bar to another. When a customer first walks into your bar, you as the bartender, should be able to tell how intoxicated they are by the way he or she approaches you, by the tone of their voice, or by their actions, especially if they are a regular. You should know that it is not polite to deny a customer's first drink at your bar. For instance, if they order a rum and coke, and you usually serve 1 1/2 oz. of rum. If they are drunk, you will want to cut back on that amount and maybe serve 3/4 oz. just to maintain a level of respect. Then asking them to have a glass of water, or soda water and lime to balance out their level of alcohol. You really don't want your customers passed out around your bar. Be patient as long as possible before asking the security to escort them out. During the process you may have shorted the customer a couple ounces of rum so next time this person comes into your bar on a normal level, surprise them with a nice strong drink. That will keep the customer happy and coming back.

Clothing

Being a bartender, from the first day on the job you must be presentable. You should strive hard to look your best. If a uniform is issued to you then fine, if not then you must present yourself respectably.

Black pants and a white shirt is standard across the board. The more presentable you are the more respect you get from you employer and your customers. (This, of course, does not apply for a beach bar).

{MALE} hair neatly cut, face clean shaven, nails properly cleaned and it is more presentable to wear a shirt with sleeves.

Drummin at the Bar

Lost & Found

What to do with lost items in your bar that you find? Notify the D. J. of the lost items. The D. J will then announce the lost items. For example: "Anyone lost a set of keys?" "Please check with bartender Kirk because if there is any reward it should be given to the finder of the item." If there is no D. J. place the item on your bar shelf at the highest point or where it is most visible to everyone. If someone comes to claim an item of value they will need to describe something personal about the item that only they would know. For example, if it is a purse ask the customer to name 3 things inside the purse. Even if a reward is involved please follow this advise.

Jr. & Barracuda for Dinner

Removing a Glass or Bottle

On a slow night while attending your bar, if you look over and see a customer's drink is low you, naturally, go over and see if they need a refill. If not, try not to remove the glass or bottle from in front them right away; if you do, the person will probably leave. If you don't move the glass there is a 50% chance that they will order another drink. On a busy night you may want to clean up quickly to maintain a steady flow of customers to the bar.

Loud Customers

How to control loud customers? For instance, let's say 2-3 people are sitting at the bar arguing a point and by their loud behavior they are interrupting others. You as the bar-tender can often balance that situation by simply turning up the music slowly to a point that everyone can only hear the music.

Substitute Liquors

All these cocktails are designed to enhance your skills as a bartender. You as a bartender will soon know more-or-less how each liquor tastes and smells. As you will run out of a particular liquor on occassion you will need to be able to substitute for them to the best of your knowledge. Try to keep the consistency of the cocktail and to keep the cocktails flowing around your bar without much noticable change in their taste and presentation.

Floating Liquor

Most professional bartenders use the back of a bar spoon to float their liquor and liqueurs on top of each others. An example would be a B52 shot. Put a 1/4 oz of Kahlua in a shot glass, then place the back of the bar spoon inside the shot glass down to the level of the Kahlua, pour 1/4 oz of Baileys on the back of the spoon slowly lifting the spoon up while pouring.

Place the spoon back into the shot glass to the level of the Baileys and then pour 1/2 oz vodka on the back of the spoon slowly lifting it up to create a B 52 shot of layers.

Here is my personal advice on how to eliminate the spoon.

Take a 1 oz shot glass in one hand and a bottle of Kahlua in the other. Put the Kahlua in the bottom of the shot glass, using the counting technique that you have already learned.

Then take the bottle of Baileys, lean the shot glass with the Kahlua until its almost spills and then put the bottle of Baileys to the rim of the shot glass then slowly pour 1/4 oz of Baileys on the top of the Kahlua while lifting the shot glass slowly to avoid spilling. At this point you should have two layers, 1/4 oz Kahlua and 1/4 oz of Baileys on the top.

The 1/4 oz of Baileys should now be at the of the rim of the shot glass where the Kahlua was. In the same position pick up and place the bottle of vodka on the rim of the shot glass slowly pour until the glass is full and ready to be served.

For your first couple of attempts at this, try NOT to talk and avoid being distracted while going through this process. Over time you will find yourself using this technique effortlessly and looking cool while doing it.

Music

I have explained before how to play your music. Playing
your music changes a bit if there is a live band performing.
You will need to think about how you play music between
sets. When the band is ready to play, you need to turn off
your stereo. But at the same time, you need to be ready to
provide music as soon as the band takes a break.

You must consider the type of music the band is playing and
how many people were dancing to it, because when you
change the music you don't want to over ride or under play
the customers. For instance, if the band is playing a soft
reggae then you might like to play something faster than
what the band was playing.

Another example would be that if the band was playing
something fast and people were dancing, then you would
want to play something a bit mellow. Always keep in mind
the condition of the customers, fast music will dehydrate
them, so by playing something soft it will calm them down
and they will be coming to your bar to satisfy their thirst.

My Area, Belize & Language

As you know, Belize is very diverse in language and culture. We use English as well as Creole, Spanish and Garifuna, often a mixture of all four. You will find that some people can take pieces of these languages and make sentences which only a Belizean would understand and can have a conversation.

Now Belize is more into tourism like never before. As a bartender you will find yourself interacting with all sorts of tourists on a regular basis. When this happens you will feel the need to master the English language and other languages that you commonly are exposed to and doing that seems to be challenging for a lot of our people. My personal advice on the English language is to learn it on the job from your English speaking customers by using words and sentences you hear from them. Don't be afraid to turn around and use the same sentence to another customer. By doing this you will be interacting with your customers more frequently, and over time you will find that you are more fluent. Then you will find yourself answering to your customers in the same manner that they talk to you. For instance "May I have a beer please?" or "Gimmi wa beer" or any other language that is common around, you won't hesitate and think what to say by doing this, you are automatically a better Bartender.

As you have learned when dealing with tourists, you need to have excellent public relation skills which also means that you need to have a lot of patience. You will often find one person that will approach you with the same question over and over, and over again especially if the question is about one of our own heritage sites, it might make you a little bit edgy answering the same question. Keep in mind to be polite at all times, and by answering the same question it will make it easier for the next similar customer you won't have to think about the same answer, you will know it automatically.

Closing the Bar

How to close your bar? You should start to get ready about 20 minutes before you want to close. To do this, announce to the people sitting around that this will be the last call for the night. If you are in control of the music start playing slower music such as nice slow reggae souls or Bob Marley and then some souls. This will then put your customers in a relaxed mood and then slowly turn up the lights. The gesture of turning up the lights will signal to your customers that it is time to leave, the bar is closing.

Kirk's Bar Tools

As a bartender now you will know that there is a whole line of bar tools out there that are designed to help you with your work. From my experience, over time, some of these tools actually slow you down, and speed counts a lot to make you efficient. So I have narrowed down and substituted some bar tools as well as learned to use the closest thing in sight to get the job done. By substituting bar tools it makes you look cool, smooth and professional while working and will catch the attention of the customers right away.

Tools you will need:

A blender or two
Bottle opener
Cork screw
Jiggers
Bar shaker
Sharp knife
Champagne stoppers
Small ice box
Garnish tray
Salt and pepper shakers
Ice scoop

A blender is used to make all my frozen cocktails. A second blender will help on those busy nights when you have multiple orders of frozen cocktails and you won't have to wait until the first one is finished to start the second.

Bottle opener, most bars have their bottle openers on the cooler or a screw on the inside of the bar, this is very efficient but slow. My choice is a bottle opener that you can hold in your hand, this way you will be able to open 5 beers on top of the cooler in less time than you can open one on the side or open a beer on the move.

Cork Screws are used to open wine. Do yourself a favor and get a good heavy-duty one. Too many are made that are cheap. Nothing is worse than having the screw part bend or break when you screw it into the cork. Be sure to screw it all the way down, if not the cork may break halfway and you may not be able to get the cork screw back in it.

At this point, you need to remove all the pieces of cork then take a pen/pencil and press down on the cork left in the bottle forcing the cork inside the bottle. Then take a long straw, place half inside the bottle with the cork and bend the straw over the top and pour the first drink—not very professional.

Jiggers, are very handy on bottles that are frequently used, they will increase your speed and give you peace of mind when pouring a drink so that you don't over-pour. If you don't have jiggers stick to the counting technique you have already learned, remember the counting technique will only work if the bottle has a manufacturer's pouring device on top.

Shakers are used to shake a drink that just needs to be chilled and not frozen. Once you have shaken the drink you remove the cover and then place a strainer on top to avoid ice falling into the serving glass. I prefer to use two disposable glasses, one with ice and ingredients and one empty. Pour one into the other 4-5 times then place the two glasses together rim to rim. Be sure to use one hand while the glasses are tight and pour into serving glass. The disposable cups replace the shakers and are easier to clean up.

Sharp knives are used to prepare your drink's garnish. My personal view on the bar knife is don't take it out of the bar for any reason, don't give to anyone over the bar counter, and if a customer asks to borrow the knife to peel an orange or some other project, don't give it to them, it's better if you offer to peel the orange yourself. Never lend the bar knife—they tend to grow legs and run away from home.

Champagne stoppers, after opening a bottle of wine or champagne use the champagne stopper which goes inside the bottle and preserves the remaining contents.

Small ice box which is used to store your serving ice. Don't forget to always use an ice scoop, don't use your hands.

Garnish tray is used to keep your diced fruits in and it must be covered at all times. Don't be afraid to use garnish with your drinks. You garnish according to the fruity ingredients in your cocktail: Piña colada has coconut cream, pineapple juice, cream and rum, etc. so you garnish with a slice of pineapple and a cocktail cherry on top. If you are out of a particular garnish use your best judgement.

Salt and pepper shakers. Always keep salt and pepper shakers close, you will be surprised how often you need them.

Kirk's Personal Bar Stories

On my first arrival at Tobacco Caye I introduced everyone to my Fireball Shot and how its effect starts within ten minutes. No one believed me that one shot could get you drunk that fast. One evening Mr. Mark and I were sitting at the bar. He was between the cushioned bar stool on the leg rest. As for myself I was behind the bar counter as usual. Then up came my friend Jay Jay and I started to tell them about this Fireball Shot I have. Of course, he didn't believe me. So Mr. Mark said "okay give him one to see if it works" and after five minutes Jay Jay said "this drink is not working!" then he jumped up to walk off when, like a mighty rushing wind behind, blew him over and he was falling. Luckily Mr. Mark was there to catch him when he fell. That's when this drink became famous and started to come alive. Everyone wanted to try a shot and everyone had different effects. People from neighboring islands came over to the bar to simply try the Fireball Shot. And that's when I made my mark on Tobacco Caye as a bartender.

Captain Doggy & The Fireball Shot

One evening Captain Doggy came from Dangriga with some guests to drop them off on Tobacco Caye. Then he came by the bar and said: Aha! I heard about this Fireball Shot I'm going back alone to Dangriga right now and I want to try one! So I mixed up a shot and he drank it then he went out on the dock jumped in his boat and headed back towards Dangriga. Later ... according to him, he missed the entire 'bar mouth' and headed the boat up the beach at full throttle. Up until this very sad day I can't sell or give him another Fireball Shot ever!

Blacks, Burk, Gordo & the Fireball Shot

My friend Blacks and his girlfriend came to the bar one evening in his boat. They came by the bar and had a couple beers with me. About 7 pm he said "I'm going home, give me a Fireball Shot!" "I want to try it!" So I gave him a shot. He jumped in his boat and headed off to Twin Caye. Later, according to him he circled around Tobacco Caye range and Coco Plum Island for about three hours and he couldn't find Twin Caye which, by the way, is the neighboring island to the left of Coco Plum when you head in a south-western direction. He is another victim of the Fireball Shot to whom again I cannot sell another! I just don't understand why folks don't trust me anymore!

'Burk' came one night from South Water Caye. After having a shot he was doing karate moves standing on the picnic tables. Again, sad to say, he's another person who cannot drink another Fireball Shot ever! Nowadays whenever I mention about the Fireball Shot, everyone at the bar just backs away! Lol.

One evening my friend Roberto went to the Coco Plum Island Bar and had a few drinks with the bartender there and started arguing about which island has the best bartender. So about 8 pm, after that bar closed up, they all got in a boat and he said to them, "I'm gonna show you where the best bartender is at!" They then headed to Tobacco Caye, they all came to the bar and had a few drinks and again started arguing about who is the best bartender. So Roberto said "Kirk give these guys a Fireball I'll pay for it!" So I said "okay."

Now Gordo is a big strong guy and he knows about the Fireball effect so he said "no, none for me." The bartender from Coco Plum said "well I am a bartender I can drink anything!" I made the Fireball Shots: one for the bartender, one for his friend and one for his barback man and served them all at the same time. Within ten minutes the bar back guy fell asleep at the bar on his stool. The other guy dropped off his stool into the sand "duup!"

Now here is I when I started to panic, I started to lock up the bar, everyone was dropping like weary birds around me! Then since Gordo is the strong one he started to pick up the guys one by one and took them back into the boat. The bartender was the strongest of the three he started cursing, jumping and shouting! By the time Gordo came back to the bar the bartender's body was dancing around he said to Gordo "don't touch me I can make it on my own to the boat." he was staggering on the dock as he tried to walk out on his own. Up until this day he's at Coco Plum asking people for the Fireball Shot recipe but I guess he'll simply have to buy my book!

Johnny Jackson's Joke

My good friend Johnny Jackson walked into my bar, sat and had a rum and coke. As he sat there, he began telling me a very 'bad' bar joke so, as a long-time bartender, I paid attention keenly, digesting every detail. Then he left and as a bartender I had to get him back with a joke too. When he came back twenty five minutes later, I took the same joke he gave me, turned it around, twisted it up a bit. He was laughing and puffing until he brought tears to his eyes and when I saw that it brought tears to my eyes. I stepped back and said "man, this is the same joke you told me twenty minutes ago." Then he really burst out in laughter so I had him mad as hell, laughing and crying at the same time. He looked at me and said "Kirk you're a real f......!"

Fight Night

One night working at the club called Pub Abnisa. It was a very busy night and a bar fight started in front of the bar with seven guys beating a man and the entire club went wild. This one guy taking on these seven men fighting them with whatever he could get his hands on chairs, bottles, pool sticks, and tables. Blood was everywhere mostly on the bar counter so grabbing a rag I started cleaning it off the bar as quick as I could then up came a customer to the bar and all I could say to him was what can I get you sir? and from then on the drinks kept flowing like nothing went wrong.

Oreo

A Canadian friend came in one night with his new catamaran which was a super boat. Two or three other boats accompanied him. They all came ashore, mixed with the folks that were already there, and the party started. I might have even served him a couple of Sneaky Kirk Specials. Two of the local gals took him to the dance floor (see photo). Somebody yelled "OREO" and instantly the whole crowd started chanting "Oreo!, Oreo!" to the music. He could actually dance pretty well—for a white guy!

Kirk's Exotic Island Bar Grub
Bar snacks

These should always be spicy or salty to make the customer thirsty which will increase drinking.

Limes—50% of your garnish tray should consist of lime slices. Limes keeps the level of alcohol in your body down and your stomach settled. Also prevents Scurvy!

Every now and then you will find a customer with an upset stomach; squeeze a half (½) of lime in a glass with soda water and ice. That will be a big help.

Ceviche

1 lb Conch diced into small pieces
1 lb Fresh peeled shrimps diced into small pieces
1 medium size mango diced into small pieces
4 large sweet peppers diced into small pieces
2 large cucumbers diced into small pieces
10 strips of cilantro diced into small pieces
2 habanero peppers diced into small pieces
3 tsp pepper sauce
Juice of 8 limes
Juice of 2 oranges
A pinch of salt {to taste}
1/4 tsp Black pepper
1/4 tsp Cayenne pepper
1 1/2 oz 151 over proof rum

Mix all ingredients in a large bowl and marinate for 15 min.
Serves 40 people. Serve with corn tortilla chips.

Bar Boca Mango

6 large Mangos sliced and diced into small pieces
Juice of 2 limes
1/4 tsp Black Pepper
pinch of salt {to taste}

Mix all ingredients in a large bowl. Serve with tooth picks.
Serves 15 people.

Bar Boca Original Shrimp Ceviche

Peel 1 lb fresh shrimp and dice into small pieces
2 large onions diced into small pieces
2 large sweet peppers diced into small pieces
5 cucumbers peeled and diced into small pieces
1 large tomato diced into small pieces
2 Habanero peppers diced into small pieces
Juice of 6 fresh limes
1/4 tsp Black pepper
Pinch of salt {to taste}

Bar Boca Cucumber Boca

6 Large cucumbers peeled and diced into small pieces
Juice of 2 limes
1/4 tsp Black pepper
Pinch of salt {to taste}
3 tsp Pepper sauce

Mix all ingredients in a large bowl. Serves 15 people. Serve with tooth picks.

Bar Boca Original Ceviche

1 lb conch diced into small pieces
2 large onions diced into small pieces
2 large sweet peppers diced into small pieces
1 large cucumber peel and dice into small pieces
5 straw cilantro diced into small pieces
1 large tomato diced into small pieces
2 habanero pepper diced into small pieces
Juices of 6 fresh limes
1/4 tsp black pepper
Pinch of salt {to taste}

Mix all ingredients in a large bowl. Marinate for 25 min. Serves 15 people, serve with corn tortilla chips.

Bar Boca Popcorn

1/2 lb Popcorn
1/4 lb Stick Butter
1 tsp Salt

Serves 15 people. Salty Bar Boca popcorn will increase bar sales and it will make the customers thirsty.

Kirk's Party Punchs

Kirk Westby
Baby Shower Cocktail

Take 1 fresh pineapple, peel, cut into four slices from top to bottom and remove the center core. Dice into small pieces, place into a blender, fill with water, blend slightly then pour into 3 gallon container then add: 5-10 spice seeds
1 qt vodka
1 qt dry white wine
Marinate for 45 minutes to an hour. After marinating add 2 liters sprite
Stir and serve over ice. (serves 20)

Kirk Westby
Wedding Party Love Potion

1 qt Baileys
7 cans natural milk
1 can condensed milk
1/2 tsp cinnamon powder
1/2 tsp nutmeg powder
2 tsp vanilla
1 qt brandy
Pour all ingredients into a 1 gallon container, shake well and serve over ice. (serves 20)

Kirk Westby
Baby Shower Cooler

2 qts white wine
1/2 qt vodka
1/2 qt dark rum
5 oz Grenadine or cherry syrup
2 liters Sprite
Put all ingredients into a 2 gallon container stir and serve over ice. (serves 15)

Kirk Westby
Apple Cinnamon Wedding Ball

Dice 15 fresh apples into small pieces and add:
2 tsp cinnamon powder
2 tsp nutmeg powder
3 bottles apple concentrate
2 qt 151 over proof rum
1 qt vodka
1/2 pound brown sugar
2 1/2 gallon water
Put ingredients in a 5 gallon jug, let marinate for 3-4 days then strain and serve over ice. (serves 30)

Jaeyleh Westby House Party Melon Ball (adults only)

Take one whole fresh 20 pound watermelon place in an upward standing position, cut a triangle on top of the watermelon about 2 inches wide. Then use the handle of a kitchen fork to plow inside the watermelon 15-20 times to soften the watermelon's inside without penetrating the outer wall. Take a bottle of 151 over proof rum, remove its cap and place the mouth of the bottle inside the watermelon at which point you should see tiny bubbles rising up inside the bottle, this means that the alcohol is slowly fusing with the watermelon. When the bottle is empty stir 5-6 times with your fork then place the bottle back as a cover, after 45 minutes to an hour later and you may begin to serve over ice.
This will ensure a hyper and successful house party. A wheelbarrow may be necessary to help get the guests home! (serves 15)

Kirk Westby House Party Rum Punch (adults only)

1 qt 151 over proof rum
1 qt dark rum
1 qt vodka
1 qt lite rum
1 bottle pineapple concentrate
1 bottle orange concentrate
1 bottle lime concentrate
1 bottle grapefruit concentrate
1 bottle fruit punch concentrate
5 fresh oranges peeled and cut into slices
2 fresh limes peeled and cut into slices
Place all ingredients in a 5 gallon jug,
fill with water, cover then shake or stir
Let sit for 1-2 hours before serving.
Serve in 8 oz glasses
This will ensure a hyper and successful party.
Again provide wheelbarrows for transportation home.
(serves 25.)

Shania Westby Ladies Night
House Party Memory Punch

Take 1 fresh pineapple, cut off skin and cut into four
sections from top to bottom and remove center core, dice
into very small pieces, place in a 5 gallon jug then add:
1 qt coconut rum or Malibu
1 qt vodka
1 pint 151 over proof rum
1 bottle pineapple concentrate
1 bottle lime concentrate
1 fruit punch concentrate
2 gallons water
Shake or stir and serve over ice after sitting for
45 minutes to an hour.
(serves 25.)

Some just can't drink—
with the big dogs

Made in the USA
Las Vegas, NV
01 February 2023

66654460R00079